Original title:
Tropical Wonders Await

Copyright © 2025 Creative Arts Management OÜ
All rights reserved.

Author: Liam Sterling
ISBN HARDBACK: 978-1-80581-629-4
ISBN PAPERBACK: 978-1-80581-156-5
ISBN EBOOK: 978-1-80581-629-4

The Tapestry of Life in Verdant Havens

In jungles thick, a parrot squawks,
It's been eyeing that coconut box.
A monkey swings, looking quite sly,
As the iguana rolls by with a sigh.

The flowers dance, their colors flair,
While frogs croak songs without a care.
A lizard struts, all dressed in green,
Pondering who's the best on the scene.

Down by the creek, the fish play tag,
Each jump a splash, it's quite a brag.
While turtles slow with style anew,
To win the race? A dream or two!

Life's a jest in these vibrant lands,
With critters holding music bands.
So come and laugh in this lush delight,
A circus of joy, from day to night.

A Flight of Fancy Over the Sea

The seagulls gossip, what a sight,
Winging their way in flight so light.
The waves applaud with a frothy cheer,
As a crab conducts from his sandy sphere.

A fish in stripes claims to be Queen,
While a dolphin bounces, sleek and keen.
"Can you top this?" the turtle grins,
As ocean friends compete for wins.

Sunset paints the sky in gold,
As a stingray dances, brave and bold.
The corals hum an underwater tune,
Riding the currents under the moon.

In every splash, there's joy to share,
With laughter floating through the air.
So come aboard this jolly spree,
Join in the fun, it's wild and free!

Island Serenades

In the shade of a palm, I sip my drink,
A coconut falls, and I start to think.
Is it a snack or a pillow to hold?
My beach towel's now a treasure of gold.

The seagulls squawk their cheerful song,
They think the fish are doing them wrong.
Everyone's dancing, it's quite a sight,
Even the crabs are feeling alright!

Lush Dreams in Vibrant Hues

Bright parrots squawk, putting on a show,
They steal my snacks, the cheeky duo.
The sun's out shining, the vibes are neat,
While I trip over my own two feet.

A hammock swings under the lush green tree,
But instead of resting, it entangles me.
In this vivid dream, I laugh and sway,
Who knew paradise was so clumsy today?

Whispers of the Ocean Breeze

The ocean hums a funny tune,
Crabs do a conga, howling at the moon.
The tide comes in with a splash and a boom,
As seahorses giggle, filling the room.

Sandcastles crumble, the waves make a joke,
A fisherman's hat flies, oh what a poke!
Shells scatter laughter across the shore,
In this breezy chaos, who could ask for more?

Sunlit Canopies and Hidden Gems

Under the sun, I found a cave,
Thought it was treasure, but just a rave!
Turtles were dancing, oh what a sight,
I joined in laughing, it felt just right.

With a map in hand, I looked so bold,
Only to find it was all just sold.
But with those views and flavors so sweet,
I'd trade it all for more fun on my feet!

Soliloquy of the Rustling Leaves

In the breeze, the leaves do dance,
Swapping gossip, they take a chance.
"Did you hear about that cheeky crow?"
"Yeah, he stole my snacks, what a show!"

Swaying branches, a leafy choir,
Whispering secrets, never tire.
"I just spotted a squirrel's hat!"
"Oh dear leaves, we're all quite fat!"

Journey to the Heart of Serendipity

Packed my bags with snacks galore,
But left my map, oh what a bore!
Chasing butterflies on a whim,
Found a beach with a coconut swim!

A tour gone wild, as I misplaced
Those directions—it's quite the chase!
But then I laughed and flipped my hair,
My journey changed, no time to care!

Heartstrings of the Sunlit Palms

Palms blowing softly in the sun,
Belly laughs 'til the day is done.
"Did you see that lizard slide?"
"He should be in the Olympics, wide!"

Sunshine tickles, it makes me giggle,
As I dance around and do a wiggle.
Palm leaves shaking to the beat,
This warm breeze can't be beat!

Mirthful Mornings in Coastal Bliss

Morning waves bring joy and laughs,
Seagulls squawking like they're in casts.
"Grab your breakfast, it's quite a feast!"
"Was that a crab? Or just a beast!?"

Sand castles sprout, complete with moats,
Where jellyfish wear tiny coats.
Every chuckle, every splash,
In this funny world, we make a bash!

Chronicles of Sun-drenched Days

In the sun's warm embrace, we laugh out loud,
Trying to tan, but looking like a cloud.
Ice cream drips, we race for a cone,
While seagulls plot to steal our throne.

With sand in our shoes and joy in our hearts,
We dance on the beach, doing silly parts.
The waves give a wave, like a cheeky friend,
And our shenanigans, they never end.

The Imprint of Barefoot Wanderers

Barefoot troopers marching on warm sand,
With jellyfish fears and a bucket in hand.
Splashing and slipping, giggles abound,
As flip-flops fly off, oh, how they rebound!

In the wild coconuts, we seek our prize,
But they just mock us with elusive cries.
Our footprints fade, but stories stay bright,
Of laughter and mischief that dance in the light.

Skyline of Palm Fronds Against Twilight

Palm trees sway as the sun says goodbye,
We wave to the bats and pretend to fly.
The sky a canvas of pinks and gold,
While we make up tales that never get old.

The breeze tickles us, a playful tease,
As we trip over roots with the greatest of ease.
Under this painting, we laugh till we cry,
And hope the chocolate sun doesn't say goodbye.

Secrets of the Whalesong

Deep in the ocean, where secrets sway,
The whales sing tunes to start the day.
We eavesdrop from boats, our ears in a twist,
Wondering if they've got jokes on their list!

With each song, a splash, and a bubble of cheer,
Like underwater parties, we start to cheer.
If only we knew what they're really about,
Maybe they'll teach us how to dance, no doubt!

Dance of the Palm Leaves

In a breeze, they're doing the twist,
Swinging their hips, they can't resist.
A coconut drops, it's a surprising fling,
The palms just chuckle, let the laughter ring.

Seagulls join in, with a squawk and a flap,
While crabs do a shuffle, no time for a nap.
In this lively scene, the sun grins wide,
As nature's silliest dance takes its stride.

Secrets Beneath the Emerald Waves

Bubbles rising, fish wearing shades,
Coral crew practicing grand parades.
A dolphin cracks jokes, as he rides the tide,
While drippy seaweed tries not to hide.

Starfish lay back, relaxing with flair,
While sea turtles trade gossip, unaware.
A clam tells a tale of the time he got stuck,
And all of the shells say, "Oh, what bad luck!"

Cascading Joys of Paradise

A waterfall giggles, splashing with glee,
Jumps into pools, says, "Come swim with me!"
A monkey swings by, with a banana in hand,
He slips on a leaf, it's quite unplanned.

Colorful flowers, each one a clown,
Throw petals like confetti, all over the town.
A parrot squawks jokes that tickle the air,
In this joyous jungle, there's giggles to share.

Echoes of a Sun-Kissed Shore

Footprints in sand, dancing with flair,
A crab does a waltz, without a care.
Kids build a castle, complete with a moat,
While a seal bounces by, on a floating boat.

The tide comes in, with a splash and a cheer,
Waves laughing together, drawing you near.
As the sun starts to dip, painting skies so bright,
Even the stars join the party tonight.

The Elysium of Gentle Rains

When raindrops dance on my head,
I wonder if they're misled.
They splash on my face, what a sight,
It's nature's way of joining the fight.

The puddles wait with open arms,
As I leap in with all my charms.
Each splash a giggle, oh what fun,
I'd call it chaos, not stormy run.

Yet clouds above twirl and tease,
Like they're in on some huge tease.
They rain on picnics, not on boats,
Just delivering laughs from fluffy coats.

Harvest Moon Over Glittering Waters

Oh look at that moon, it's quite the show,
Shining bright, like a disco of glow.
Fish dance below, under the beams,
While ducks quack away, it seems they're dreams.

I tried to catch one, right by the shore,
But splashes and giggles? I caught much more.
The clumsy moonbeams slipped on the tide,
And slipped on my shoes, oh where's my pride?

So I'll keep laughing, as the sun makes way,
For another night of antics and play.
The waters glimmer with tales to tell,
Under the moon's watchful, funny spell.

Mirage of the Oasis

In the middle of hot desert sun,
A mirage appears, oh what fun!
I see a pool with umbrellas and shade,
But alas, the heat's made another charade.

I grab my canteen, a sip and a laugh,
Where's the palm tree? It's just a gaffe.
The sand tickles my toes in delight,
My oasis is gone, but the fun's in sight.

In every grain, a new game unfolds,
A treasure hunt for water that's bold.
I'll build my own with buckets and flair,
And float in dreams saved from the air.

Breath of the Ocean at Midnight

The ocean whispers secrets so sweet,
At midnight, it plays a tricky beat.
Waves crash softly, like chuckles of fate,
As crabs do a dance, oh isn't it great?

A jellyfish glows like a lantern in the dark,
Lights up the shore, with a goofy spark.
I trip on a shell, and roll in the sand,
Laughing at how life is so well-planned.

The stars above wink and giggle along,
While fish in the deep hum a silly song.
The ocean's breath, a ticklish delight,
Keeps the midnight funny, 'til morning light.

Beneath the Canopy of Kaleidoscope Dreams

In the forest, monkeys swing and sway,
Dropping coconuts in a messy display.
Parrots shout jokes in vibrant hues,
While sloths take naps—they're snooze-day blues.

Lizards wear shades, they strut with flair,
Chasing each other without a care.
A frog in a hat croaks out a tune,
Under the light of a smiling moon.

Luminescent Nights Among the Foliage

When fireflies disco in the warm, soft air,
I trip on a root, good thing I'm rare!
The frogs cheer me on with a ribbiting song,
While I ponder how I got this wrong.

The palm trees sway like they're at a ball,
While a raccoon sneaks snacks, oh, he's got gall!
Bamboo pipes serenade with a sound so neat,
As coconut clowns dance to a zesty beat.

A Symphony of Colors at Dawn

In the sunrise glow, the toucans dance,
While the iguanas plan their nightly prance.
Bamboo stalks play flutes, oh what a show,
As the sun spills orange, pink, and a glow!

A gecko in tights leaps high on a crate,
Thinking it's cool—but we think it's great!
The bees join in, buzzing off-key,
As the flowers all giggle, sharing some glee.

The Heartbeat of the Ocean Breeze

Waves crash like laughs upon the shore,
Seagulls squawk jokes, who could ask for more?
A crab with a cape scuttles with pride,
Claiming the beach, taking it in stride.

Sunburnt tourists tumble and trip,
While dolphins perform a splashy flip!
The breeze carries giggles from the sand,
As everyone dances to the ocean's band.

Mirage of the Coral Gardens

In the coral depths, fish dance around,
Wearing hats made of seaweed, what a sight found!
Octopus in sunglasses, lounging so bright,
Turns to a crab—"Hey, don't steal my light!"

Starfish play poker, odds truly absurd,
With shells as their chips, bluffing unheard.
A seahorse snickers, "This game's on a roll!"
While the jellyfish glows, the life of the shoal!

Radiance in the Rainforest

In rainforests shady, the monkeys conspire,
To steal every fruit, they'd climb even higher!
Parrots tell jokes, with beaks full of flair,
While sloths move so slowly, they forget where they stare.

"Knock, knock!" says the toucan, perched on a vine,
"Who's there?" chirps a frog, with a leap and a shine.
The leopard just grins, tail flicking with pride,
Watching the chaos with laughter inside.

Hidden Treasures of the Coast

Along sandy beaches, crabs have their dance,
They scuttle and scurry, it's quite a strange trance!
Seashells are treasures, but they can't hold a tune,
As waves tease the seaweed, under the moon.

The gulls shout "Mine!" as they snatch up some fries,
While a starfish sidles, wearing a disguise.
"Is it a bird, or a fish?" they burst out in shouts,
With laughter and mirth, the shoreline rejoiced with clouts!

Enchanted Isles and Moonlit Nights

On islands so bright, the coconuts giggle,
As crickets serenade with a silly wiggle.
A glowworm winks, "I'm the party's spark!"
While tiki torches flicker, lighting up the dark.

A turtle with shades moves slow but quite cool,
"Why rush?" he chuckles, "I'm nobody's fool!"
The waves clap their hands, in a friendly charade,
Where sea creatures joke—nature's own parade!

The Call of Wandering Winds

Winds whisper secrets, oh what a hoot,
Palm trees are dancing, in their funny suit.
Hats fly like kites, what a silly sight,
Chasing coconuts feels just so right.

Sandy toes giggle, as they wiggle around,
Seashells play tag on the warm, sandy ground.
Something smells odd, a coconut stew,
Or maybe it's just my new foot odor too!

Serene Sunsets Over Gentle Seas

Sunsets can't help but blush pink and gold,
While seagulls crack jokes, oh, they're so bold.
Fish in the sea, with smiles on their fins,
Cheering the sunset, as day softly spins.

The horizon yawns, oh what a big stretch,
Crabs hold a concert, no one would dare fetch.
With sandcastles crumbling, they lose their cool,
"Next time," they mumble, "let's build with a tool!"

Revelations Under a Starlit Sky

Stars twinkle, giggle, and share their bright dreams,
While crickets compose silly midnight themes.
The moon pulls a prank, on a wandering cloud,
"Hey you!" it shouts, "Get lost in the crowd!"

Fireflies flicker, putting on a great show,
Dancing with laughter, while shadows take flow.
"Catch me if you can," they tease with a grin,
As I chase their glow, my patience wears thin!

Harmony of Colors in Paradise

Bright colors collide in a vibrant mess,
Birds sing in chorus, without any stress.
A parrot takes selfies, with a goofy pout,
"Look at my feathers!" it sings out with clout.

In this canvas of mirth, laughter does bloom,
While turtles break dance, making room in the gloom.
With paintbrushes swirling and laughter we bring,
In this paradise place, joy is the king!

Melody of Waves on Soft Sand

The ocean sings a sandy tune,
With crabs that dance beneath the moon.
A seagull drops its chips with glee,
As jellyfish wave, 'Come join the spree!'

The beach ball bounces, wild and free,
While sunscreen's slathered, just like brie.
Flip-flops fly in a silly race,
As laughter echoes, we find our place.

Echoes of a Hidden Paradise

In a jungle gym of vines and trees,
Monkeys giggle with the buzzing bees.
A toucan sports a bright, bold hat,
While squawking turtles beg for a chat.

Lost in green, we twist and twirl,
As sloths hang low with a sleepy furl.
The parrots squawk, their voices loud,
Creating chaos that makes us proud.

Wildlife Chronicles of a Forgotten Cove

Where dolphins leap and otters slide,
The fish parade with colorful pride.
A crab throws shade with a claw in hand,
While sea cucumbers just as planned.

Electric eels throw a shocking dance,
As jellyfish float in a lazy trance.
With snorkeling gear, we swim and weave,
In a tangle of seaweed, we laugh and cleave.

An Odyssey Through Cascading Waterfalls

With every splash, a hilarious tale,
As turtles glide and rafts set sail.
A frog jumps high with a froggy cheer,
While fish jump up, 'Come join us here!'

Water lilies giggle in the breeze,
While dragonflies dance with such ease.
We slip and slide on the slippery rocks,
In the giggly depths, time truly mocks.

Mosaic of Flora and Fauna

In a jungle where the monkeys play,
Flowers dance in the sun each day.
Parrots squawk their colorful tune,
While the sloth sleeps like a lazy balloon.

Lizards wear their finest hats,
Dodging the curious chattering rats.
Bees buzz with a silly cheer,
While the iguana sips on fresh cold beer!

The orchids giggle, looking quite sly,
As butterflies flutter like they can fly.
Tigers grin with a crafty smile,
Plotting to rest for a good long while.

In this paradise, no worries at all,
Not even a frown, we're having a ball!
With joyful pranks around every bend,
Nature's laughter will never end.

Secrets Hidden in the Underground Rivers

Beneath the surface where the water flows,
There's a party where no one knows.
Fish wear hats, and eels wiggle in glee,
Touting their tales of a wild jamboree.

Crabs in tuxedos dance on the rocks,
Planning a heist with their clever clocks.
While turtles bake pies in a curious style,
All giggling at their own little guile.

The current whispers jokes as it swirls,
Tickling the whiskers of tiny squirrels.
With bubbles of laughter that rise to the light,
The gossip in waters is quite a delight!

Oh, what could be hiding just down below?
Adventures await, as fast as a flow.
But watch your step, or you may just find,
A fish in a bowtie, so sweet and so blind.

Charm of the Weathered Shoreline

Where the sand meets the sea so bright,
Seagulls perform in a comical flight.
Crabs wear shades and strut like they're cool,
While the starfish learn to swim in the pool.

Seashells clamor, they gossip and cheer,
Trading the latest beach gossip here.
Waves tickle toes with splashes of fun,
While the sun plays hide-and-seek, oh what a run!

The rocks wear hats, all mossy and green,
They argue and bicker, a funny scene.
As dolphins dance with a flip and a flop,
The ocean waves laugh until they stop.

So grab your bucket, come join the spree,
The shoreline spills secrets as wild as can be.
With treasures aplenty and giggles galore,
The charm of this place will leave you wanting more.

The Adventure Beyond the Coral Reef

Under the waves where the fish tease,
Jellyfish float with utmost ease.
Clownfish giggle, hiding in holes,
While shrimp throw parties, shaking their shells.

Dolphins leap like they're on a stage,
With seals who mime in a silly rage.
Turtles plot their next grand tour,
While octopuses juggle, a real ocean score!

Coral castles built with flair,
Home to creatures both bold and rare.
With a wink from a puffer, and a wink back,
This underwater world never lacks.

Join the merry dance of the undulating tide,
Every bubble, a secret, a joy to confide.
The colors, the laughter, a splash in your heart,
The adventures in waters set you apart!

Celestial Skies Over Glittering Shores

Breezes whisper secrets of the sea,
While crabs dance like they're on a spree.
Palm trees sway with swagger and cheer,
Sunsets come in colors that most don't wear.

Starfish lounging, laughing out loud,
Seagulls forming quite the rowdy crowd.
Flip-flops flapping, a silly parade,
Footprints washed away, what a charade!

Coconuts roll down the sandy lane,
Chasing each other like a wacky train.
Sandy toes with a side of crabs,
Beach life unfolding like comic jabs.

Laughter echoing, a comical show,
As waves crash in, putting on a glow.
Everyone's dancing without any care,
Mischief on the shore is truly quite rare.

Lush Canopies and Crystal Waters

Vines are swinging from left to right,
Monkeys throwing coconuts, quite a sight!
Frogs croaking wildly, still quite a tune,
While flowers giggle at the cream-hued moon.

Mangoes drop like laughter from the trees,
Parrots squawking jokes, only they can see.
Squirrels in shades, sipping on bright juice,
Thinking it's the height of wild abuse.

Wading through waters that sparkle and gleam,
Fish full of mischief, plotting to scheme.
Ducks quack in rhythms, a strange serenade,
In this lush paradise, silliness won't fade.

Glinks of sunshine dance on surface brights,
Pineapples wobble in jovial flights.
Each splash a story of vibrant mirth,
In this land of laughter, the garden of Earth.

Silhouettes Against a Golden Horizon

Surfboards gliding like birds in disguise,
Board shorts flapping, oh what a surprise!
Flip-flops strutting down the sandy way,
Chasing the sunsets, calling it a day.

Kites soaring high with a giggling twist,
Caught in a gust, as if they insist.
Seagulls in shades, posing for the show,
Waving goodbye as the sun starts to bow.

Shells hold secrets of playful pranks,
Waves form teams in their splashing banks.
Sun-kissed laughter paints skies so bright,
What a spectacle, oh what a sight!

Laughter echoes, mingling with the tide,
As moonlight whispers, come join the ride.
In shadows we dance, taking it slow,
As golden horizons bid a soft glow.

The Dance of the Hibiscus Bloom

Hibiscus swaying, with a twist and twirl,
Dancing like it knows how to unfurl.
Bees buzzing in, they just can't resist,
Making mistakes, it's a pollen-filled twist!

Butterflies fluttering with silly grins,
Navigating petals where the laughter spins.
They tumble and roll through lively air,
Creating a scene like a colorful fair.

Sun shines brightly, casting playful beams,
Poems form in the air, like whimsical dreams.
Breezes giggling like they know the score,
In this floral realm, we can't help but adore.

Every flower opens, shares a delight,
Blooming with laughter in the warm sunlight.
Join the parade, let your heart take flight,
In this joyous garden, everything feels right!

Bamboo Groove Beneath Starry Skies

In the grove where shadows play,
Bamboo sways in a cheeky way,
Monkeys swing with a playful grin,
While fireflies dance, let the fun begin!

Stars above twinkle with glee,
As laughter rolls like a salty sea,
Crickets chirp a merry tune,
Echoing joy beneath the moon.

A lizard blushes, all dressed in green,
Sipping nectar from a flower's sheen,
Frogs in bow ties croak jokes on the spot,
Life here is silly; life's a whole lot!

Grab a coconut, sit back and think,
Should I dive in or just have a drink?
In this groove, mischief brews,
Adventures lurk in the evening hues.

Enigmatic Tides and Moonlit Paths

Waves giggle as they kiss the shore,
Secrets hide in their playful roar,
Starfish chuckle with each gentle splash,
While crabs scuttle in a clumsy dash.

Tides whisper tales of treasures lost,
While moonlight covers the sand like frost,
A dolphin tricks, leaps high with cheer,
Flipping over waves, the show is near!

Shells wear hats in a vibrant parade,
With jellyfish waltzing, such a charade,
The beach is a stage for creatures bold,
Telling their tales, both silly and old.

So grab your champagne and raise a toast,
To the nightly show we love the most,
Where laughter bubbles and sparkles blend,
Under moonlit paths, fun knows no end.

The Language of Parrots and Palm Trees

Polly wants a cracker, but holds a chat,
In a grove where palm trees don't know where they're at,
Parrots yap, squawking lines like pros,
In jokes that only they seem to know.

Nuts fall from trees with a plop and a bounce,
While iguanas bask, with a smug little flounce,
Sunshine giggles like it's in on the fun,
While the toucan struts; it's a colorful pun!

Every leaf rustles in a gossip spree,
As nature laughs at all who can see,
The rhythm of life in this laughing abode,
Is where humor flourishes, forever bestowed.

From chattering parrots to trees so quaint,
Each day begins like a joyful paint,
With colors and chuckles, oh what a tease,
In this happy dance of palm and breeze.

The Essence of Paradise in Every Breath

On a sunny day, the scents arrive,
Coconut breeze makes us feel alive,
Frangipani giggles with sweet delight,
While the sun dips low, painting the night.

Every inhalation brings laughter anew,
With mangoes tumbling just for you,
Papayas whisper jokes on the tree,
As butterflies flutter, oh, can't you see?

Palm fronds fan fables of joy untold,
In every gust of wind, stories unfold,
The waves join in with a playful woosh,
As our hearts sway in a loving roosh!

In this paradise, each breath is a gift,
With giggles and glee, we simply drift,
So savor the moments, let laughter reign,
In this essence of joy, we all gain!

Rippled Reflections of a Sunlit Dream

In a hammock strung high, my drink's in a can,
A parrot steals snacks as my plans go all 'man'!
The sun is a spotlight, my woes are awash,
I dive for a mango, but instead, get a squash.

Jellyfish dancing, they prance quite bizarre,
Trying to tango, but they just raise the bar!
A crab in a bowtie, he winks at my chair,
He'd offer a dance, but he'd rather not share.

Flip-flops are slipping, my feet start to slide,
As seagulls are laughing at my joyful ride.
In paradise here, all's a comical scene,
The lunacy flows like the waves in between.

Mirrored reflections of merriment sheer,
In this sunlit adventure, I've nothing to fear.
With laughter as currency, I'm rich in delight,
As the day turns to dusk and the stars shine so bright.

Whispers of the Surf and Sand

The surf shouts secrets in gurgled delight,
While sandcastles giggle, holding on for a fight.
A turtle in shades, sunbathing for fun,
He's the local celebrity, oh what a run!

Seagulls are critiquing my beachside buffet,
One swoops in close, steals a fry, oh hey hey!
Shells whisper stories of surf and good cheer,
As the tide pulls a prank, it's all so sincere.

My beach ball's deflated, a sad little lump,
Yet still, I find joy in this warm, silly jump.
Shells make fine jewelry with laughter as glue,
In this sandy escape, there's just me and you.

Whispers of joy ride the waves to the shore,
Every salty giggle's an open door.
With antics and fun floating right on the sand,
Life's a big chuckle in this whimsical land.

Daybreak on the Happy Isles

Sunrise brings laughter, a color parade,
Palm trees are dancing, they're never delayed.
Coffee spills over from hands oh so clumsy,
The beach chair's a throne, but it feels quite flimsy.

Lime slices wobble upon cocktail's embrace,
A crab wears my sunglasses with marvelous grace.
Joggers look serious as they pick up their pace,
But a pelican swoops down, it's all such a race!

The dew on the grass is like pearls in a row,
As I frolic through blossoms, all covered in glow.
Nature laughs softly, the breeze is a tease,
Ballet of the breezes puts my mind at ease.

Daybreak is silly, a marvelous jest,
In this vibrant haven, I've found my sweet nest.
Laughter and sunlight combine in a cheer,
In the happy isles, I'll always draw near.

The Artistry of Nature's Canvas

Nature's a painter with colors so wild,
She splatters the skies, like a mischievous child.
Brushstrokes of laughter dance under the sun,
While creatures in chaos remind us of fun.

A flamingo struts in a tutu—so bold,
Her antics are stories that never grow old.
The ocean's a canvas, with waves seeming grand,
Where starfish and seaweed cling hand in hand.

Palms sway like dancers, they twirl and they spin,
While a wind-chime's laughter gets pulled from within.
Rainbows jump out from the clouds up above,
As every mishap embraces the love.

Artistry flourishes, a scene pure and bright,
With giggles and splashes, it feels just so right.
In this whimsical world where silliness reigns,
Nature giggles softly, adorned in her gains.

Enchanted Shores of the Forgotten Isles

Seashells giggle on the sand,
While crabs dance in a merry band.
A pineapple wearing shades so cool,
Invites us all to join the pool.

A parrot jokes from a tall palm tree,
"Are you here for laughs? Come swim with me!"
Flip-flops flapping, we race the tide,
As fish swim by, their scales full of pride.

The sun's a jester in the sky,
With cotton candy clouds drifting by.
Seagulls play tricks with our packed lunch,
Stealing chips in a sneaky crunch.

Laughter bubbles as we explore,
Waves tickle toes along the shore.
Every moment's a comedy show,
In these forgotten isles, we steal the show!

Bounty of the Mangrove Maze

In the mangrove maze, we take a stroll,
Where mudskippers leap and twirl like a pole.
Snapping turtles wear funny hats,
As we chase the rhythm of dancing rats.

Beneath the roots, an otter grins wide,
Saying, "Come join my aquatic ride!"
With mud and giggles, we slip and slide,
Our laughter echoes, we cannot hide.

The mangroves hum a silly tune,
Even the crickets join the croon.
Butterflies wink, wearing polka dots,
In this wild maze, we forget our thoughts.

As the sun dips down and fireflies zoom,
We gather 'round, making our own room.
Each twist and turn has endless glee,
In the mangrove maze, we're wild and free!

The Call of the Wind Through Coconut Trees

The coconut trees whisper and sway,
"Hey, don't forget to laugh today!"
A breeze tickles our sun-kissed skin,
And dancin' palm fronds invite us in.

Swaying bodies, we mimic the scene,
Coconut shells are our makeshift screens.
Laughter and gales combine in a cheer,
As we twirl about, we lose our fear.

A monkey shimmies on the branch so high,
"Join the fun or else I'll fly!"
With each gust, we spin and glide,
In this leafy circus, we take pride.

Underneath the coconut shade,
We share jokes and lemonade.
Every swing brings a joyful blast,
Embracing the wind, together we last!

Sunsets Bathed in Tropical Fire

The sunset spills like melted gold,
As we sit here, away from the cold.
With turquoise drinks and hats askew,
We laugh at the sky in fiery hue.

The palms wave like they know the score,
While we swap stories, always wanting more.
Each sunset dance is a funny sight,
Our shadows skip into the night.

A crab's reviewing our funny moves,
Scribbling notes as if to prove
That joy becomes a vibrant spark,
As day gives way to a whimsical dark.

With giggles echoing, the fireflies gleam,
In this luminous landscape, we dare to dream.
As the stars pop out like flaming sparklers,
We savor life as ultimate chucklers!

Journey Through Vermilion Horizons

A parrot stole my sandwich, what a cheeky bird!
He squawked and danced, not a care in the world.
I thought I'd share my picnic on the sand,
But now it's a buffet for my feathered friend!

Palm trees waving like they've lost their minds,
Frogs wearing sunglasses, oh what a find!
The beach ball bounces, then takes a dive,
While jellyfish practice their jiggly jive!

Hammocks swing low, now that's pure delight,
Until a crab pinches me, what a fright!
With laughter echoing, the sun shines bright,
We'll surf the waves till it's time to bite!

Sunscreen's a must, but not on my fries,
Wild ants throw a party, oh, what a surprise!
Each wave brings a giggle, a splash, and a cheer,
Living the dream, oh, it's nearly beer o'clock here!

Unraveling Mysteries in Lush Groves

In the jungle, I tripped over my shoelace,
A tortoise chuckled, what a slow-paced race!
Monkeys throwing berries, what a breakfast delight,
They must think my hat is their favorite sight!

Lizards in sun hats swap gossip so loud,
While flowers gossip, oh, aren't they proud?
Squirrels in tuxedos dance on the ground,
Their nutty ballet beats all that I've found!

The creek sings a tune that's catchy and sweet,
While hippos attempt a water ballet feat.
Hiding behind bushes, I try to compose,
But it's hard not to laugh at a frog in repose!

Oh, who knew that nature could be such a jest?
With creatures conspiring to give me a test.
In the depths of the thicket, it's never a bore,
Every day's an adventure, & just wait for more!

Surrender to the Lullaby of Nature

A lullaby plays while crickets tap dance,
Fireflies twinkle, it's a magical chance!
The breeze tells secrets through palm tree leaves,
While frogs sing sweetly, oh how they tease!

Grasshoppers jumping like they're on a spree,
On daisies they bounce, quite merrily!
Dolphins in the distance leap high and cheer,
"Join us," they whistle, "the fun is right here!"

Under the stars, I lay with a grin,
Listening to stories as the night settles in.
The moon's so goofy, plays peek-a-boo light,
While kids with glow sticks make the darkness bright!

With laughter and giggles, sleep hugs the air,
Nature's a comedian, it's everywhere!
As morning arrives, with my dreams in a spin,
I can't wait for tomorrow—let the hilarity begin!

The Abode of Majestic Creatures

In the forest realm, with a bunny in boots,
Claiming he's king, while the rooster salutes!
Flamingos in pink prepare for a show,
Waltzing and prancing, putting on quite a glow!

A rhino on roller skates rolls down the lane,
While a sloth throws confetti, it's hard to explain.
Kangaroos are juggling with bananas in style,
And the sun bears laugh, it's a party worthwhile!

The giraffe's doing yoga to help with his stretch,
"More leaves, more fun!" says the parrot's sketch!
Elephants trumpet tunes as they chug along,
Jungle's a concert, a chaotic, wild song!

With critters conga dancing beneath the bright trees,
Nature bands together, oh, how they tease!
A festival every day, come join the delight,
In this home for creatures, everything feels right!

Songs Carried by the Cotton Candy Sky

Up in the sky, a sweet delight,
Fluffy pink clouds, a sugary sight.
Lollipops dance on a breeze so light,
Sugary dreams take off in flight.

Jellybean showers, candy rainfalls,
Marshmallow giggles echo through walls.
Gummy bears ride on the wind's calls,
As laughter blooms where sweetness sprawls.

Frolicking fruits in a joyful spree,
Bananas in boats, oh what a sight to see!
With sprinkles of sunshine lighting the spree,
The sky winks down; it's wild and free.

Catch me a cloud, I'll wear it right,
Flip-flops in hand, ready for flight.
Sipping on joy, from morning to night,
In a world spun sweet, everything feels right.

In Praise of Forgotten Islands

Hidden away where quirks abound,
Islands of laughter, they spin around.
With coconuts wearing little crowns,
And crabs that dance in their silly gowns.

No maps will lead you to this place,
Just follow the giggles, pick up the pace.
Sloths play chess with a relaxed grace,
While seahorses twirl in a slow embrace.

The sky's a palette, wild and bright,
As pineapples sing in pure delight.
With every wave, there's a splashy fight,
And all the sea creatures join the night.

Come find the joy in every nook,
To the rhythm of nature, we're off the hook.
With every breeze, laughter's the book,
On these wild shores, let's take a look.

Beneath the Silver Veil of Night

Under a blanket of sparkling skies,
The moon cracks jokes, oh how it tries!
Stars wear shades, looking quite wise,
While the night whispers funny goodbyes.

Fireflies twinkle like disco balls,
As owls give wisdom from their lofty halls.
The waves clap hands, their laughter calls,
Join in the fun as daylight falls.

Shadows frolic by the pale moonlight,
With giggles dancing, a joyous sight.
Even the crickets join the night,
Singing tunes till morning's first light.

Come wander where the silly things roam,
In the silver night, you're never alone.
In the laughter of night, we find our home,
Under stars, our hearts freely comb.

The Pulse of the Shoreline

At the shoreline, where giggles clash,
Waves tickle toes as they splash and dash.
Seashells whisper secrets in a flash,
While sandcastles rise and then crash.

The tide comes in with a frothy cheer,
Carrying tales from far and near.
Seagulls squawk jokes about their sphere,
As we laugh and play, it's all sincere.

Surfboards sail like laughter's flight,
Tanned with joy, it feels just right.
With sunscreens smeared and hats held tight,
We dance on waves, night's edge in sight.

Feel the pulse where the land meets blue,
With happy moments that spark anew.
In every ripple, laughter breaks through,
At the shoreline, it's just me and you.

Between Blossoms and Waves

In a hammock tied between two trees,
I spotted a crab, dancing with ease.
A coconut fell, oh what a sight,
The dance turned to chaos, pure delight.

Bright flowers bloomed, they waved to the sun,
I joined their party, oh what fun!
A parrot squawked with jokes so bad,
I laughed so hard, my sides just sagged.

The waves rolled in, a playful tune,
As I donned my hat, a flower boon.
Flip-flops slipped, I made a splash,
A fish winked at me, then made a dash.

Between blooms and tides, now it's a spree,
Who thought paradise would be so zany?
With sandy toes and a goofy grin,
In this joyful chaos, let the fun begin!

Mysteries of a Hidden Lagoon

In a lagoon where secrets hide,
A turtle winked, he took it in stride.
He offered me a ride, what a deal,
But I fell off, oh the fish did squeal!

The water sparkled, not just with sun,
It giggled and bubbled, oh what fun!
I asked the reeds for a good chat,
They whispered back, 'Don't bother the cat!'

A crab in a tux talked of the tide,
With pinchers that clicked, he seemed so spry.
He told such tales, I laughed till I cried,
While a clam just sat there, feeling bona fide.

In this hidden nook, where wonders rush,
Even the seaweed joined in the hush.
With laughter echoing, I swam away,
To seek more mischief in the salty bay!

Island Whispers

Whispers from palms tell secrets true,
Like why the coconuts wear a shoe.
The breeze carries giggles, sweet and light,
As crickets sing jokes into the night.

A monkey in shades swung by with glee,
He offered me snacks, a banana spree.
I shared my chips, but he took the whole bag,
Now I'm left crunching, feeling a nag.

Under the stars, the island speaks,
The waves share tales of tropical peaks.
With laughter and snacks, we dance quite bold,
Swaying to rhythms the night unfolds.

In these whispers, the night takes flight,
Where every moment is pure delight.
So join the fun, don't miss the chance,
On this island, everyone gets to dance!

Serenade of the Sapphire Sea

The sapphire sea sings a tune so bright,
Its waves make me twirl, in pure delight.
A seagull swoops by, with a cheeky grin,
'You can't catch me,' he seems to spin!

The sand tickles toes like a playful friend,
As shells tell stories that never end.
I named a starfish, Sir Fuzzy Feet,
He waved back at me, so very sweet.

A crab's playing chess with a witty shrimp,
They argue and laugh, but not a blimp.
Under the sun, their rivalry's grand,
While I just munch snacks, sun-soaked on sand.

In this sea of laughter, with shades so fine,
Every wave tells jokes, every ray does shine.
Join the serenade, let your spirit soar,
In this laugh-filled paradise, who could ask for more?

Wanderer Among Giants of Green

In the jungle, I trip and I tumble,
A toucan laughs as I watch my stumble.
The vines are thick, a real twisty maze,
I'm led by a squirrel who's plotting my ways.

The trees loom high, like nature's tall friends,
With leaves that dance, making shadows that bend.
Then comes a sloth, who moves ever slow,
He shrugs at my pace, saying, "Just go with the flow!"

Monkeys swing by, with their cheeky chimes,
Stealing my hat, oh, what silly crimes!
Their chatter a symphony, wild and absurd,
While I chase my belongings, looking quite bird.

Yet in this green world, with laughter and cheer,
I find joy in chaos, that's ever so clear.
For every misstep, there's a giggle to catch,
As I wander among giants, unplanned, just a match.

Festivities Under the Canopy Stars

The night ignites with firefly laughter,
As critters gather for the wildest chapter.
An owl flips pancakes, quite a sight to behold,
While raccoons debate if their dance moves are bold.

The moon is a disco ball, shining bright,
With birds in tuxedos, taking flight.
A frog plays the bongos, giving a beat,
While ants form a conga line, feeling the heat.

The party goes on, with thrills and delights,
As pineapples toast with coconuts' heights.
A parrot DJ spins tunes with great flair,
And everyone's grooving, not a worry or care.

In this savory scene, our joy is no fable,
We feast on fruit salads, all decked at the table.
With laughter and cheer, under starry displays,
These odd festive moments, we'll cherish always.

Kaleidoscope Dreams on a Pristine Beach

The sun flares up, like a pop of confetti,
As crabs strut by, all dressed in spaghetti.
The waves launch a tickle, pulling me near,
Where fish do the salsa without any fear.

I build a grand castle, with shells piled high,
A seagull swoops down, with a mischievous eye.
He snatches my snack, with a chuckle and flap,
While I'm left giggling, a soft sandy clap.

In the distance, a dolphin leaps gleefully,
Shooting fish at friends, oh what a spree!
As kids splash around, with buckets in tow,
They're hunting for treasures, a colorful show.

So let's bask in this charm, under sun's warm embrace,
Where laughter and joy spread a magical space.
With every grain of sand, a memory to make,
In kaleidoscope dreams, laughter won't shake.

Serenades of the Nestled Coves

In a cove so snug, where the waves sway low,
A crab gives a concert; his fan club says 'whoa!'
The fish hum a tune, with bubbles that pop,
While sea stars do the limbo without a stop.

The sun dips down, painting skies with delight,
As the laughter of dolphins dances in flight.
The sand grains chuckle as toes dig in deep,
While a turtle sings lullabies, gentle and steep.

With shells as our tambourines, we sway in the breeze,
As the moon joins the party, gliding with ease.
The whispers of water serenade the night,
In this cozy cocoon, every moment feels right.

So here in the cove, with wonders and cheer,
Every creature's a dancer, bringing smiles near.
In the ripples of laughter, we all find our voice,
Singing sweet serenades, in this peaceful choice.

Dappled Sunlight on Emerald Leaves

In the jungle where the monkeys swing,
Fiddleheads dance and crickets sing!
The sun plays tricks through leafy screens,
While lurking frogs plot their funny schemes.

Sipping nectar, bees do a jig,
Worms wear tiny hats, oh so big!
Lizards laugh as they slip and slide,
Caught by a parrot with a funny pride.

Dancing shadows on the forest floor,
Who knew nature could be a chore?
The breeze carries giggles with a twist,
As butterflies join in a wacky tryst.

So when you wander where the wild things roam,
Pack a laugh, no need to moan!
With dappled sunlight, be ready to greet,
A comedy show, all nature's treat!

Secrets of the Coral Kingdom

Beneath the waves, fish wear a glee,
Dancing about like they own the sea.
Coral castles, with doors that stick,
Enter if you dare, but watch out for a trick!

Octopuses juggle with giddy delight,
While starfish compete in a dance-off fight.
Whales hum tunes that echo quite loud,
They're auditioning for a sea creature crowd!

Sea turtles trade gossip with flair and flair,
While crabs wear their shells like a fashionable pair.
Bubble-blowing fish share their best tales,
Of bubblegum pranks and funny scales.

In the kingdom where colors collide,
Expect the silly on every tide.
Secrets are plenty, but laughter is key,
For a dive in this realm is the best, you'll see!

Vibrant Echoes of the Rainforest

In the wild where the wild things chatter,
A parrot squawks, 'What's the matter?'
Bamboo shakes with giggles and glee,
As creatures plot their next antics with tea.

Howler monkeys put on a loud show,
While frogs in tuxedos leap to and fro.
The jaguar grins, oh what a tease,
Sipping rain from the vines with ease.

With every rustle, a joke's taking flight,
A sloth's slow dance steals the limelight.
Echoes bounce, as colors ignite,
In this jungle, everything feels just right.

So when you roam where the tall trees sway,
Pack your humor for a sensational stay.
In this vibrant land, where echoing laughter plays,
Joy is abundant, in surprising ways!

Beneath the Palm's Embrace

Under palms, where the coconuts drop,
Squirrels skedaddle with a comic hop.
Sandcastles rise, then promptly collapse,
With waves that giggle, and friendly slaps.

Chasing after shadows on a sunny plot,
A crab in a hat claims the best spot.
Seagulls squawk jokes from above the shore,
As sunbathers roll and tumble for more.

In flip-flops and sunglasses, we frolic and cheer,
Barefoot adventures—there's nothing to fear!
With every chuckle, the warmth does expand,
In life's sandy playground, let's make a stand.

So join the fun as the day slips away,
Beneath palm fronds, where laughter holds sway.
In this shimmering haven of sun and embrace,
There's joy in each moment, a perfect race!

The Symphony of Nature's Palette

In the jungle, monkeys swing,
A melody of chirps they bring.
Parrots squawk in colors bright,
Nature's band, what a delight!

Lizards sunbathe on a rock,
Tickling toes as the clock ticks clock.
Bamboo claps in gentle glee,
A symphony of wild jubilee!

Even the sloths join the song,
They're slow, but they won't be long.
Swaying to a breezy beat,
Grooving on with wobbly feet!

So let us dance the day away,
Filled with laughter, come what may.
In the colors, in the sounds,
A joyful never-ending round!

Blossoms Above Crystal Waters

High above the sparkling sea,
Butterflies flap with pure glee.
Flowers wave from shores so near,
Saying, 'Hey! Come see us here!'

Frogs croak jokes as fish swim by,
While the sun paints the azure sky.
Shells giggle and tickle toes,
As sandcastles rise like prose!

Seagulls dive for crumbs with flair,
As beachcombers hunt without a care.
Each wave whispers secrets old,
In laughter and joy, we're consoled.

Balloons float, quite out of reach,
While crabs practice a beachside speech.
Nature's antics never cease,
In this realm, we find our peace!

Luminous Horizons at Dusk

As the sun dips down to rest,
The sky wears its colorful vest.
Fireflies twinkle like tiny stars,
While crickets play their guitars.

Colors blend in a funny way,
Making shadows come out to play.
Even the moon winks with a grin,
Saying, 'Let the night begin!'

A parrot sings in a silly tone,
As the world turns to a relaxed zone.
Laughter echoes in the air,
As owls hoot without a care!

Every dusk brings its own delight,
A carnival of giggles at night.
Join the dance, be part of the fuss,
In the glow, we gather, all of us!

Kaleidoscope of Exotic Aromas

Whiffs of mango float through the air,
Bringing smiles to faces, showing flair.
Pineapple and coconut swirl around,
Creating joy, laughter abounds!

Spicy scents from grilling food,
Tickle noses, putting them in the mood.
Aromatic breezes dance through trees,
Making everyone say, 'Oh, yes please!'

Curry clouds and grilled shrimp cheer,
As everyone gathers near.
Laughter mingles with every taste,
In this feast, there's no time to waste!

From every corner, flavors collide,
In this banquet, we wear our pride.
Savor the moments, take a bite,
In this aroma-fueled night!

www.ingramcontent.com/pod-product-compliance
Lightning Source LLC
Chambersburg PA
CBHW072132070526
44585CB00016B/1635